The Path to Creativity

Creative Writing Exercises
to Awaken the Artist Within

Copyright © 2013 Charity Hume

All rights reserved.

ISBN-10: 149361178X
ISBN-13: 978-1493611782

Cover artwork from Claude Monet's *The Covered Path*
Book Design by Glynnis Kashtan

CHARITY HUME

THE PATH TO CREATIVITY

Creative Writing Exercises
to Awaken the Artist Within

WRITING HARVEST

LOS ANGELES

There is a vitality, a life force, an energy, a quickening that is translated through you into action, and because there is only one of you in all of time, this expression is unique. And if you block it, it will never exist through any other medium and it will be lost.

- Martha Graham

CONTENTS

1	Introduction	1
2	Lost and Found	5
3	Missing Person	7
4	Your Favorite Character	11
5	Kryptonite	13
6	Point of View	15
7	It's Elemental	17
8	Mirror Mirror	19
9	Family Photograph	21
10	Haunted House	23
11	Food Glorious Food	25
12	Flashback	27
13	The Interview	29
14	Tools of the Trade	31
15	Family Story	33
16	Road Trip	35
17	The Return	37
18	The Turning Point	39

19	Bluebeard's Room	41
20	Innocence	43
21	Fevers	45
22	Bliss	47
23	Snakes, Spiders and Bats	49
24	The Refuge	51
25	Pictures From a Magazine	53
26	The Betrayal	55
27	Hiding Place	57
28	Liar Liar	59
29	Pas de Deux	61
30	True Wealth	63
	Acknowledgements	65
	About the Author	67

INTRODUCTION

Pathway in Monet's Garden at Giverny - Claude Monet

This past summer I went to France after many years away, and I was able to immerse myself in the Impressionist masterpieces in the great museums of Paris. The first day we arrived I met a school group and took a tour of Giverny, Monet's gardens not far from Paris. Our crowded tumble through the flowering beds and colorful gardens gave us a feast for the eyes, and we took hundreds of pictures of the glowing flowers. Only later, in Paris, did I fully understand that they had been carefully recreated from the documents of Monet's paintings, faithfully continuing his vision of their wild riot of color. Inside Monet's house, the walls, the paintings, the colors of china and furniture continued this visual fantasy. It was luscious. For lunch we went to a restaurant a few steps down the road, called "La Ferme," which has been in operation since the days when Monet and Jean Renoir would come for a glass of Sancerre. A warm, poetic light fell on blond, wood-paneled walls, and glinted from the glasses, a light that had inspired Renoir to paint his friends at the same table a century ago. In Paris, I stood in homage for hours inside the walled room of water lilies in The Orangerie, an oval room where one can experience in 360 degrees a world of color stretching out from a single point of view, in Monet's incredible continuous circular painting of a pond that reflects the light and depth of the sky on its surface. It is an experience of such poetry I said to my son, "This room is why I brought you to Paris."

The Impressionists whose paintings are accompanying these exercises were students of observation. It is possible to view over fifteen hundred paintings Monet and Renoir did over the years of their career, 1500 each. If one looks at them chronologically, it becomes clear that Monet would go to the same place and paint the same scenes and subjects over and over again, at different times of day, altering in tone, mood and meaning. For Monet, painting was a daily practice.

These writing exercises are meant to give writers of all ages, from beginners to those who have published work, an inspirational "practice" of the art of writing. These exercises are like a musician's "etude," or a painter's subject. Each can take you to the heart of your own vision, because they draw from the unique material of your own memories and autobiographical experiences. They will allow you to explore your own identity, and they will give you the footage you need to create the work that is waiting to be expressed within you. Jack Kerouac once wrote, "Something that you feel, will find its own form." Like Monet and his garden, you can return to these exercises over and over again. You will find that they awaken different moods and results on different days. You can make a quick sketch, or spend time enough to develop a longer work, depending on the material each one elicits within your own memory. Get ready to experience your own Giverny. As you write, enjoy the feast of color on the path to creativity.

LOST AND FOUND

Japanese Doll – Boris Kustodiev

Make a list of some of the things you ever loved and lost. Start anywhere, a little toy you remember, a favorite t-shirt, your childhood nightgown with the roses embroidered on the collar. Go through the rummage sale of your mind and remember them, and fill a page with the things you bring to mind. Whenever you feel the urge, expand on the item and explain its importance, its physical shape, color, texture, condition when new, when lost. When the page is full, read it over carefully, and underline the sentences about your favorite remembered lost item, or circle it. One or two will have stories connected to them, so tell the one that calls your name.

On a fresh sheet of paper, or a new "document" in your PC, write about this object in particular, and about any ideas or memories that surface as you begin. There's no pre-conceived form for this exercise, but you may discover this simple object may give you a story to tell. Take your time and enjoy the adventure. You will "find" something you lost.

THE MISSING PERSON EXERCISE

The Pink Dress – Frederic Bazille

All of us have people in our lives who populate the corridors of our memory. In this exercise, think of a person that you are no longer in contact with. The person could be "missing" in any sense of the word: a childhood friend who moved away, a teacher from long ago, someone you knew who died, a relative you never met, someone you wish you could forgive, a friendship you outgrew. First write down the list of possibilities. One name on that list will have the greatest emotional "charge" for you, or spark an internal response as you look at it. Circle the name and write it down on the top of a blank piece of paper.

Once you commit to one "missing person," write down everything you can remember about him or her. Think of any detail, any fragment of conversation, any texture or place you associate with this person. Here are some questions to consider:

> Where do you picture this person in your mind?
>
> What is your first memory of him or her?
>
> What did he or she look like?
>
> What did he/she wear?
>
> What smells, tastes, sounds are registered in your memory?
>
> What dialogue snippets come to mind?
>
> What are some of the more dramatic things that happened?
>
> What feelings begin to surface?

Use concrete, physical details as you record your memories. Rather than using abstract descriptions, "It was a beautiful apartment," mention the brass doorknocker that was shaped like a pineapple. Write until you exhaust all the information in your brain about this person. Maybe you can tell us about the way the fridge was organized, or how the idea of stewed green beans with peanut butter sauce really grossed you out. The point is to put it all in. Every memory we have was recorded through the sensations of taste, touch, sight, smell and hearing. Use the five senses in a kind of check list. When you get to hearing, mine your mind for the things said, and even harder, what was never said. When you are done with the process of remembering, it is possible that you will already have the rough draft of a story. I have worked with writers who began this exercise and wrote a novella by patiently returning to write about the same person over time. Give yourself time to fully mine your memory for the treasures you have stored away.

YOUR FAVORITE CHARACTER

Claude Monet Reading – Pierre-August Renoir

Think of all the books you've really treasured, and write down a list of characters that you most related to at different times in your life. Think of the books you couldn't help rereading as a guilty pleasure, knowing you were just having the same old experience, but were unable to resist. When you have a few of these characters in mind, try some of the following exercises, by assuming the identity and point of view of the character you've chosen from your reading. If you're more of a movie buff, choose a character from a film, or a person from a portrait in a museum. As long as the pull on you is personal, and real, you'll have a good candidate to try some of the following:

> Write a poem, (or a series of poems!) based on the experiences of your character.
>
> Write a first person monologue in the voice and point of view of your character.
>
> Write a missing chapter that explains this character's life more fully.
>
> Write a screenplay of your favorite scene in this book.
>
> Research art connected to your character or the world described in the novel. For each image you find, write a commentary that explores the connection you see between the story and the art.

KRYPTONITE

The Desperate Man – Gustave Courbet

In the comics and movies about Superman, he is invincible, except when he is in the presence of "Kryptonite," an element from his home planet that has the power to weaken him. In each of us, there are certain memories, phrases, and addictions that can cause us to crumple into our weakest selves.

Create a character in a story with a secret weakness. Think carefully about ways to contrast the inner "Kryptonite" identity with the external personality of the character. In *American Beauty*, (spoiler alert) the military father hides his attraction for men from the world. His secret weakness is so unbearable to him, he kills to avoid it coming to light. Our hidden weakness can be a dramatic motivator, luring us into the darkest place. Or it can be a dream that takes us to the stars, as it does in *October Sky*, when a miner's son dreams of being a rocket scientist but is too fearful to share his hope to escape the drudgery of his father's life. Either way, the tension between the inner and outer sides of character will give you rich material.

POINT OF VIEW

Man at the Window – Gustave Caillebotte

This exercise is about learning to establish a consistent character point of view for the reader. It is a key tool in crafting stories. Based on the events below, tell this story from the child's point of view. When you finish a page, turn it over and write it again from the woman's point of view.

A child returns home from school, but no one is home. It is getting dark. Exiting the house, the child begins to follow a trail along a river. When the child reaches a bend in the river, he can see a woman in the distance standing on a bridge overlooking a waterfall. At the sound of her name, she turns and faces the child. They begin to speak.

Remember, you can only say, touch, see, hear, or experience reality through the medium of the character you've chosen, start to finish.

Once you have tried out this exercise, consider taking a minor character from a novel you loved, and trying on that character's point of view. In *The Wide Sargossa Sea,* Jean Rhys took a minor character from *Jane Eyre* and wrote a novella from the perspective of Rochester's first wife. John Gardner did the same in *Grendel*, when he retold *Beowulf* from the monster's perspective. Choose a minor character from a novel you love and write a monologue, poem, or chapter that explores his or her perspective.

IT'S ELEMENTAL

Onions – Pierre-August Renoir

When we observe an object from nature in its original state, whether it is a stone, a shell, or a feather, we grasp something that has had millions of years to acquire its form. A feather, when observed closely, will reveal intricate aerodynamic design, just as a grain of sand, when magnified, reveals luminous, jewel colored crystals. Paying close attention to an object from nature reveals powerful information about the formation of the universe. An astronomy professor, Barry Madore, used to ask his graduate students to spend a month examining ordinary sand. The students were disappointed, until he said, "What if this sand were from Mars?" Everything on the Earth has the potential to reveal powerful information. Your concentration will open the door.

Choose an object from nature that has not been altered by human beings: i.e. an orange, egg, rock, feather, tooth, bone or pinecone. Place the object in front of you on a table. Observe, examine, and experience the object with all of your senses: smell, peel, cut, rattle, taste, smear and crack. Write down everything you've discovered. Welcome tangents and new ideas. Let them lead you into new territory but stay with your object. Generate "footage." Finally, edit what you've written. Look for the best phrases, the strongest moments, and find the form best suited to your ideas. Was it a poem? A series of questions? The answer will vary depending on your mood. This "etude" will refine your ability to observe and discover.

MIRROR MIRROR

Marion – Guy Rose

Painters of self portraits look long and hard at their own reflections, attempting to accurately portray the changing reality each day brings to the human face. No two portraits are ever alike. When examined chronologically, these paintings express a profound evolution of artistic vision. Rembrandt, Van Gogh, Frida Kahlo, Chuck Close, Warhol, and countless others, explored their artistic message by returning again and again to the powerful exercise of creating self portraits.

Give yourself time to study your reflection in a mirror. Take a notebook along to record the ideas and observations that pass through your mind as you look. Pretend you are having a conversation with a guest and listen to what "your reflection" has to say. How are you doing? What is going on? What is on your mind? Who are you? What do you see? You can have this conversation daily. What do you most hope you could do today and why? Is it possible to make a few minutes of time for it today? Write down your deepest hope for the day. This exercise can have surprising results, because by articulating your desires, you will be more able to recognize the many opportunities that present themselves throughout the day. Doors will open.

FAMILY PHOTOGRAPH

The Monet Family at Their Garden at Argenteuil

Think of the photographs that have been taken of your family. Make a mental catalogue of these images in your mind, maybe a collection carefully pasted into a scrap book, an ancestor in a frame in the house, a Thanksgiving portrait with everyone round the table, or a First Communion snapshot, or the images of your parents' wedding. Describe a few of these with a little nametag so that you can identify them. For example: Family group shot on Thanksgiving when Clare hurt her elbow, and wasn't smiling, but everyone else is saying "cheese." Or: "Mother's wedding portrait."

For today, choose the one picture that most intrigues you. Write for twenty minutes about all the details that surround it: family stories, context, memories of the person it portrays, or the reason you never knew or met someone in the photograph. See where this journey takes you, by following tangents or associations in detail. Let the picture give you a way to focus.

You will end up with another kind of portrait, one that explores the "back story" behind that photograph.

HAUNTED HOUSE

The Old Fairbanks House – Childe Hassam

Whether it's the Bates Motel, or the stairs down to the cellar where you once saw a snake, some houses will remain with us as spooky, mysterious, or "haunted." In this exercise, use your memory to think of real places you have visited and splice together the elements that intrigued you or made you curious. Take a walk through the rooms and describe the feeling you have as you walk into this space. Try to stay physical as you write: use all the senses and give us details. Rather than write: "It was scary," describe the moment when you first spied that rusty meat hook dangling from the barn wall.

FOOD GLORIOUS FOOD

Hipp, Hipp, Hurra – Peter Severin Kroyer

Inspired by the buttery "Madeleine," Proust famously wrote *Remembrance of Things Past*, a novel that extends over several volumes, as the tastes and smells from a delicious food from his childhood began a chord of association that ultimately brought the whole of his personal history into his consciousness. Touched by food, the mind awakes.

While this exercise is not designed to begin an entire novel, you may be surprised at the wealth of associations food can awaken in your mind. Write down a list of some of the favorite foods or meals in your life. Include the people who prepared this food, the rooms where you remember tasting, smelling, sharing. Think of food you enjoyed as a child, the kind of comforts and indulgences that filled your mouth with joy. As the various memories emerge from the depths, let yourself tell a story about one of them, including descriptions of its preparation, the anticipation of waiting for it to arrive at the table, and the memory of some of the people who were there. Potentially, eating in a particular time and place can culminate in discovery, and act as an organizing motif in a story this food asks you to tell from beginning to end. This exercise can also work for food you did not enjoy. Tell the story of how you hid that calves' liver in a napkin and hid it in a potted palm in order to escape the fate of having to swallow .

FLASHBACK

Corner of the Apartment – Claude Monet

In *Casablanca*, Bogart's suave veneer of indifference to human suffering – "I stick my head out for nobody," -- is suddenly drawn aside, when he gets drunk and the film shows his flashback to Paris. We see an earlier Rick, one who believed in love, hopeful, thinking about the future. His past self explains his present bitterness and gives a glimpse of his true character.

In this exercise, tell a story of a character dealing with a situation in the present, but use flashbacks to a second storyline from the past. Find ways to tell the two stories simultaneously, giving us little tidbits along the way. Daily reality can awaken images, sights, sounds and smells from the past. Showing a multifaceted dimension of your character can be a deep way to more fully understand his or her motivations.

THE INTERVIEW

The Conversation – Pierre August Renoir

Interviews can be like treasure hunts. I was once assigned a story for a community paper that wanted an article for a tour boat. When I first began the story, I thought I was going to do a summer article about cruises for school groups. I met the captain of *Duen*, a beautiful old sloop, on a dock outside Sidney on Vancouver Island. On the brief tour of the "pilot's cabin," I noticed a small newspaper clipping, with a photograph of a group of Norwegian men during World War II. When I came home and began research on that photo, I learned that those young men were members of the Norwegian resistance. *Duen* had been part of the Shetland Operation, and the men had barely escaped Nazi capture during a crucial episode of the war. My article took a dramatic turn into history.

In an interview, think like Sherlock Holmes, and try to find the buried story. Follow the clues that lead to the richest material. Everyone, absolutely everyone, has a story to tell that would never cross your mind on first meeting. The art of finding that story, however, involves a little detective work on your part. Follow your instincts and the clues you are given to dig further. The interview is a tango, in that it takes two. Another interviewer will find a different story. Focus on the information that most inspires your interest and curiosity. Tell *that* story.

TOOLS OF THE TRADE

The Parquet Planers – Gustave Caillebotte

When I was a child, my father's barn seemed to be a world unto itself. He had a gift for working with wood, and the tools above his workbench were mysterious and intriguing; there were hand planes, wood clamps, a rip saw for cutting across the grain, and fine toothed backsaws for complex cuts. Above the bench, racks held gradually ascending sizes of wrenches, hammers, and screwdrivers. There were sandpapers of every fineness, awls and drills for boring holes, tubes of epoxy and bottles of linseed oil. A locked cabinet held toxic paints, polyurethane, and turpentine. The floor of the barn was always covered in sawdust

Watching people work tells us who they are, the confident way a mechanic gets under the hood of a car, an experienced pastry chef who rolls out a dozen tart shells with careful precision. Think of cooks, dentists, athletes and dancers. Where do they work? How do they use the tools of the trade? What are the sounds, sights, smells, textures and tastes of their daily routine? Research a profession by watching an expert at work. Out of this research, create a character portrait by describing in detail what he or she really knows how to do.

FAMILY STORY

Mrs. Cassatt Reading to her Grandchildren – Mary Cassatt

Many families have stories about intriguing relatives who have lived adventurous lives, or who emigrated from foreign lands, or who faced hardships, or personal challenges. I remember a story about my great grandmother, who lived in Colorado in the 19th century. A rattlesnake had been seen in several hen houses throughout her area, destroying the eggs, and slipping away into the darkness. A hunt was organized by all the men in the neighboring farms; they went through fields in a line, sweeping rakes carefully through the tall grasses in search of the dangerous snake. They were gone all day and came back empty handed.

My grandmother greeted them on their return at dusk.

"Go look in the hen-house," she said.

They found the snake with a pitchfork through its head. My great-grandmother had killed it earlier in the day when she heard a ruckus among the hens.

In this exercise, think of a family story that has always

awakened your interest and curiosity. Use photographs, interviews, or letters to help you learn more about the world and the people involved. Research and imagine, and begin to write. You can use this exercise as a "memoir," or an article that is historical, accurate and researched, or you can let your characters inspire you to create a fictional world, where you take on the character's point of view.

ROAD TRIP

The Road to a Particular Interest – Ferdinand Hodler

From *The Canterbury Tales*, to Jack Kerouac's *On the Road*, the transformations that happen when we hit the road and leave our daily routines behind can open a whole new dimension of experience. In the course of a journey, we meet new characters, experience obstacles and solve the challenges that unfold in the course of our journey. Road trips are not always easy. Flannery

O'Connor blends the concept of horror and social realism, along with a dash of ironic humor, in "A Good Man is Hard to Find," when she tells the story of a family road trip gone horribly wrong.

Tell the story of a road trip in all its realistic detail. Include the squabbles in the car, the arguing over who is driving, or the reflective connected silence between a parent and a child that unexpectedly bonds them after a year of fighting. Use your own memories of journeys, and tell the back stories that begin to weave their way into the narrative as you recall some of the adventures. Before you begin, think of the transformations you've experienced while you were on the road, and find the material that you think will give you the most dramatic material. That drama can be subtle, an internal "letting go" of a relationship that is over, or it can be more dramatic, Thelma and Louise on the lam. Enjoy the journey, and see where the road leads you with the characters who accompany you on the way.

THE RETURN

Moonlight, the Old House – Childe Hassam

Stories of the return are epic and magical. Odysseus endures hardships, war, obstacles and shipwreck before he ultimately evolves into the warrior who can regain his stolen home. But a return doesn't have to be from a literal journey or separation. In one of the West African folk tales about Kiriku, a child with wisdom beyond his years, a sorceress terrorizes a village until Kiriku finds out the secret to her cruelty. It turns out there's a thorn in her heart. When Kiriku removes it, she returns to compassion, forgiveness, mercy and love. A return can be one of the heart, or to a point of view one had previously discredited. A return to health after illness, or reconciliation after an estrangement, can also form the heart of a story.

What "returns" have mattered most to you in your own life?

When were you separated from those you cared about? Reflecting and taking notes on these autobiographical experiences will give you a wealth of material to explore. Brainstorm for ten or fifteen minutes. When you are done, use some of that material to write a story in which a character returns after a separation, either one that is literal or emotional.

THE TURNING POINT

Three Tahitians – Paul Gauguin

I remember hearing William Styron, the American novelist, speak at a dinner in New York; the phrase I most remember from his talk has stayed with me: "A novel is a progress toward an event, after which nothing will ever be the same again." A turning point reverses the previous world, and gives you a whole new identity. It burns up your past in a conflagration of everything you've ever known. To go on, you must forget who you were. That's a turning point. No way back.

Create a protagonist who faces a dramatic change, a place where nothing that worked in the previous world has any meaning any more. Think of turning points from novels, plays and films you've enjoyed in the past. What is the turning point for that protagonist? What scene? What moment? What forces are at work? A turning point can be revealed in stunned silence: a woman who thinks she rules the world is faced with a diagnosis of breast cancer; a star student is caught cheating on an examination; a child discovers his father's business is corrupt. All of us have faced moments that tap into this dramatic territory, choices that changed the future. Explore the autobiographical decisions you've made. If after writing on this topic, you are interested in creating a story around this key event, go for it. Give your character a chance to twist in the wind.

BLUEBEARD'S ROOM

Portrait of the Old Man – Vagan Horenyan

Bluebeard was a wealthy nobleman who lived in a beautiful castle. He had married many times, but each wife had disappeared. Wary of Bluebeard, the town maidens avoided him, but he finally persuaded a young woman to marry him. After the wedding, Bluebeard gave her the keys to all the rooms in his castle, and said she could explore them when he left the next day. But one key he forbade her to use. Of course, as soon as she was alone, she couldn't resist opening the forbidden door. To her horror, she discovered the bodies of all the previous wives, and dropped the key in fright, staining it with blood. Bluebeard returned to find the tell-tale key, but she escaped his wrath by locking herself in the highest tower until her brothers could rescue her.

In this exercise, think of a forbidden door, a forbidden act, the one thing the protagonist must not do. Create a story that shows the drama of temptation, the veneer of a life that is apparently noble or beautiful, with a dark secret hidden inside. The secret can be ordinary: a teenager's magazine stash under his bed; a mother's love letters saved in an attic shoebox for many years. The moment of discovery brings the "forbidden" into the light. Have fun setting up this story, and let the reader want to open that door before you open it for them. Begin with your own memories. What doors were forbidden to you?

INNOCENCE

Mother and Child – Mary Cassatt

Sometimes life is pure and uncomplicated. Love is just love. A child's kiss, a peaceful nap under a tree, a blissful moment at a family gathering when you realize you are having fun and there's laughter in the room. These are moments we treasure for their simple beauty. We are in the moment and need nothing more, finding a haven in the company of a friend, or feeling that rapture and peace of reuniting with a loved one after being apart.

Innocence can be fleeting, but it also suggests the unexpected surprises life offers in the midst of our busy lives.

Create a list of moments you treasure for their simple, innocent pleasure. When you've roamed the corridors of your memory for a few of these, choose one that particularly matters, and write everything you can about this memory, using your senses to recreate the sounds, sights, textures, smells and tastes you can explore as you examine the moment in greater detail. You will be surprised at how your mind has recorded details you may not have thought about for many years. Once you have your "footage," consider writing a story that includes this moment somewhere in its timeline, either as a point of departure or as the culmination of a character's experience.

FEVERS

Sick Young Girl - Michael Ancher

Novelists have sometimes used sickness as inspiration: Camus in *The Plague*, Thomas Mann in *Magic Mountain*, Geraldine Brooks in *The Year of Wonders*. Write about illness, either by researching one you have read about in an article in the media, or even better, one you have witnessed first hand, as a patient or by caring for a loved one. Illness can create a separate world that divides the healthy from the stricken. Give your full attention to the progress of the disease, its effect on the character, the circumstances and changes that result when illness interrupts the patterns of daily life. This can be a light hearted exercise, or one that is a portal into a whole world. In *To Kill a Mockingbird*,

Harper Lee subtly organizes the arc of the novel as Scout tries to remember details about the summer her brother Jem broke his arm. The point here is not to hyper-focus on illness, but to see where the "symptom" or the illness can take you.

BLISS

Couch on the Porch Summerhouse – Childe Hassam

In the movie *Groundhog Day*, Bill Murray's character is trapped in an endless repetition of his worst day. At one moment, despairing of being able to ever escape from the dull repetition of his most tedious chores, he describes a day in his memory when he was in the Bahamas, ate lobster, and frolicked in amorous freedom with a sweetheart. "

Why couldn't I have *that* day?" he asks.

In this exercise, conjure up a perfect day out of the past, finding moments that inexplicably held moments of happiness for you. Give yourself time to roam for different glimpses of bliss, and they may have been brief, but memorable. I think of a day when I looked out over the square of St. Mark's Plaza in Venice; it was a hot, windy summer afternoon, and I'd been travelling and walking, and had taken a moment to rest on some stone steps and look out at the water. The moment has stayed with me as a kind of surge of joy in just being alive filled my heart. I have found a different kind of joy when holding my son when he still let me hold him tight, the way it made me secure to know he was nearby. Think of your moments of joy, and take your time as you describe them in detail. Later, you can think of these moments as places of resolution for characters, or for an essay that explores the questions of why life matters. Construct a narrative that ends with one of your moments of bliss.

SNAKES, SPIDERS AND BATS

Flor Imperiale, Coral Snake and Spider – Marianne North

In *Indiana Jones and the Raiders of the Lost Ark*, Harrison Ford gets a laugh when after riding through Amazonian rapids, stealing a grave idol, fighting off warriors and flying through the air like Tarzan, he then confesses that he's mortally afraid of snakes. We may not all be Indiana, but many can identify with his squeamish fear.

In this exercise, make a quick list of some of the creatures that especially scare you. My list might include both objects and situations: heights, driving on the freeway, dentist appointments etc. (I could go on!) Select a phobia of the day and commit to using it. Don't waffle. Write for a page about this fear, and associate to every time you can physically remember any real encounter with this object: the day you stepped on a jellyfish, that time your mother insisted you eat okra. As you write, don't worry if there are several different memories crowding in your mind. Once you're done, you will have interesting footage. From here, you can consider a story or poem that uses your imagery and feelings. Try to be specific and realistic, as you tell the story of the cockroach you saw your first night in the Brooklyn apartment, the possum on the road, the barn spider that first week in Canada. You can also create a fictional character who shares your phobia. Write a monologue as this character explains his fear to another character, or talks to himself in an "interior monologue." Use your "footage" freely and give this fictional character a truthful side.

THE REFUGE

The Hut at Trouville, Low Tide – Claude Monet

One of my favorite "war stories" was written by Tim O'Brien, in a collection called *The Things They Carried*. A veteran of the Vietnam War, O'Brien's narrator recalls the decision to enlist, and his desire to run away from the draft. In a beautiful story told from the point of view of a scared teenager, he describes his flight from his hometown as the draft deadline nears. He finds a safe haven in an out of the way motel run by an old man with an unusual understanding and wisdom. The teenager is on the brink of an escape to Canada, considering the life of an exile from his family, his country, his past. The refuge offered in the three or four days with the motel owner creates a world where we see the pause between flight and action. These days provide us with a window into the internal choice the character has to make. We live in that refuge knowing that the clock is ticking, and the tension builds as we know that the character needs to act.

Create a situation a character who finds a safe place, a sanctuary that protects him in a difficult situation. When you start, begin with people, places, activities in your own life that have given you this refuge, and describe them in detail. What were you hiding from? What did this person give you that no one else could? When you begin with material from your memory, it is very likely you will discover the seeds for a story that will yield rich, personal material that no one but you can write.

PICTURES FROM A MAGAZINE

Shinnecock Interior Studio – William Merritt Chase

When we focus on a particular image, sometimes the results can be surprising. Our minds are full of emotional depths and stories that want to be told, and looking at art, at photographs, or concentrating on a single object, can give us a powerful way to focus.

Scan through a magazine of your choice, and tear out a page with an image that speaks to you more powerfully than any of the others. In this one magazine, it's your favorite. Concentrate on the feelings, sensations, memories and snippets of conversation that your mind remembers, as you consider this picture and let your mind both focus and wander into the associations this picture awakens in you.

Because you have a visual focus, the image you have chosen

can unexpectedly lead you to associations to the past, memories that touch on the senses and feelings in unexpected ways. You may find yourself writing in a way that is rich, layered, symbolic, and personal. Give yourself permission to "go all the way" to an emotional epiphany as you write.

THE BETRAYAL

Parau Api – Paul Gauguin

What are the most significant motivators for human beings? There are primal moments in our lives which touch on the deeper feelings inside us, and draw us into action. Moments of betrayal between husband and wife, friends or siblings, form the heart of drama. These betrayals can have small consequences, or they can be cataclysmic.

When have you been betrayed? When has someone truly let you down? When have you done the same? Write a few pages in order to explore these questions. Don't worry if intense feelings rush back as you write. Just let them flow onto the page in their raw and honest state. Later, you can edit, disguise, and fictionalize if the "true" version inspires you to use its rare, powerful material. When you have some "footage," construct a story, fictional or autobiographical, around a betrayal you know all too well.

HIDING PLACE

Hide and Seek – William Merritt Chase

I was a member of a large family, and I remember finding various "hiding places" throughout my childhood where I could get away from the busy clamor of siblings and parents and lose myself in books, reading for hours in trees, in a loft in our barn, or in a park where I had a lakeside view, but was hidden from sight. There were games we played – "Hide and *Ghost* Seek," when we looked for one another with flashlights in the dark, or "Sardines," when a group of kids gradually pack themselves into a tight spot till they are found by the last player. But hiding can also be more dramatic. I remember sneaking home way after a curfew, when I needed to get into bed without being noticed.

Think of these moments in your own life. Remember the times you may have needed to hide something: a parental illness that couldn't be shared with a younger sibling; a rendez-vous with forbidden friends who had not met with parental approval. What were you hiding and how did you avoid detection? Brainstorm as you consider different memories. Then, write a story that draws on a time when you needed to hide something, or hide from someone. It can be a light-hearted secret, or it can be a powerful moment of escape from forces larger than you were prepared to deal with at the time. Let the reader understand the sensations of the fear of discovery, the motives, the duration and tension of hiding a secret. When you work from specific memories of your own life, you will find seeds for interesting and powerful stories.

LIAR LIAR

Confidence – Pierre-Auguste Renoir

The lies we tell can reveal character and motivation. In *Casablanca*, Ilse Lund evades Rick's offer to pick her up on the way to the train, by saying lightly that she has errands to run. Only later do we realize she was trying to save his life by getting him out of Paris before the Nazis arrest him. Her lies covered enormous pain at the reality she could not go with him, and in the dramatic scene between them, a subtext of her conflict gives the scene poetic depth -- "Kiss me as if it were the last time…"

In this exercise, write a dialogue between two people, where one of them is lying to the other. Give them a setting: a kitchen, a diner, a waiting room in a doctor's office. They can be talking about the weather, or the food, but one character is covering up a secret with little lies. Plot is the art of withholding information, so there's no need to reveal the secret at the end of the scene. Just give one of your characters something important to hide, and explore the ways you can tap into that subtext throughout their conversation.

PAS DE DEUX

Dancers Bending Down - Edward Degas

The Pas de Deux is a dance for two. The great ballet duo, Rudolf Nuryev and Margot Fontayne, danced to world acclaim for many years; you can still see their famed Pas de Deux from *Romeo and Juliet* on YouTube. The dance lasts a few minutes, but it forms the heart of the whole ballet. Everything in the story depends on the crucial moment of their duet, showing the first steps toward a love that would shake their world and transform them forever. A kind of Pas de Deux can be found in stories and plays as well. In the famous American play *Our Town*, George and Emily go into an ice cream store. At the beginning of the scene, they're two teenagers talking about homework and high school. At the end of the scene, the audience knows that they have pledged themselves to one another for life.

Write a dialogue between two people that expresses a close relationship between them. Your people don't have to be lovers. Think of different archetypal pairs: parent-child, mother-daughter, father-son, etc. Pairs can be boys exchanging secrets in grade school, or two office workers realizing the boss embezzles funds. Once you have your two characters, write down what they say to one another in "real time" as you listen to the characters begin to interact, not with you, but with one another. Surrender as they begin to play verbal tennis. Watch and listen. You're the scribe.

TRUE WEALTH

Nurse Reading to a Little Girl – Mary Cassatt

Make a scrapbook, either in a computer document, or by using a notebook. On each page write the name of a different person. If possible, find or create an image of the person you are describing and paste it under the name. If you don't have an image, skip that phase and go straight to the following: Be free and think about people who've given you something important through the example of their words, their actions, their artistic and human legacy. Later on, you can include anyone particularly inspiring from public life, but begin by thinking of people you know personally who have helped you better understand your true nature, your purpose, your potential, or your dreams. Allow yourself to be forgiving if there are few people who come to mind at first, and be happy if there are many. Give yourself permission to recollect the words, phrases, physical details and memories that give you this "charge" of happiness, centering, or understanding and write them below the pictures. The points of connection, contact, and communication with individuals throughout your life will begin to come to you. As you mine your mind for the treasures you've buried within for so many years, you will discover your true wealth. Dig.

ACKNOWLEDGMENTS

I am indebted to many people for their help in writing *The Path to Creativity*. Together, they form the creative, collaborative community that made it possible. Hoyt Hilsman, Adam Leipzig, Bob Goldstein and Connie Nassios, have each played a crucial role in helping me publish and connect to a larger community by generously giving me their encouragement, expertise, and guidance in the past years. While many others have also given me support, I wanted to recognize the contributions of several people who have given hours of time to help this book come to fruition.

Glynnis Kashtan, graphic designer, has believed in this book from its first creative moments. When we collaborated on *The Wisdom in the Room*, her visual pairing of art with creative writing exercises began a series of discussions that ultimately led to *The Path to Creativity*. I can't thank her enough for her generosity, commitment, patience and expertise. Glynnis' countless hours of research, design, and programming, her encouragement, and her thoughtful editorial advice made *The Path to Creativity* possible. Above all, I am grateful for her faith in the meaning and value of this kind of book.

Kim and Michael Harrison, co-founders of *Socratica*, continue to guide me with their experience and creative counsel. I am thankful for their friendship, their generosity in editing, and for the ways in which their trail-blazing into on-line education has inspired my own work.

Ann Diederich is a constant companion in my creative process, and some of these exercises are directly inspired by our conversations. I am thankful for her intellectual generosity, and for her encouragement, guidance and expertise in planning our trip to France. The art I experienced on this trip allowed me to think about how all of us can encounter the creative vision within.

My husband Don Neill generously and tirelessly contributes to my writing identity in the daily creative exchange that makes up our life together. I am indebted to him for the constant support he gives me in so many forms. His wisdom and insight, his willingness to brainstorm and fine tune, and his reassurance in hours of doubt, inspire me on the path we are both taking to realize our creativity together. I remain grateful, in love, inspired.

ABOUT THE AUTHOR

CHARITY HUME is a writer, and a teacher with over thirty years of classroom experience in independent schools. Hume is a graduate of Yale University and received an M.A. in Creative Writing from NYU, where she was awarded a prize teaching fellowship. Hume returned to NYU in 1992 as director of the graduate creative writing program. While there she produced the NYU Creative Writing Series and wrote and administered a grant from the New York Times Foundation to initiate a partnership between NYC public school teachers and The New York Times Teaching fellows. She has published her work and commentary in journals and periodicals in the United States and in Europe. She was a radio co-host for *The Winds of Change*, a weekly spoken word program in Canada, and continues to contribute to *Cultural Weekly*, an online magazine for the arts. She is presently a dean at The Polytechnic School in Pasadena, California.

Made in the USA
Columbia, SC
05 July 2024